the Rock of Doubt

Sydney Carter

Continuum
The Tower Building
11 York Road
London SE1 7NX

15 East 26th Street
New York
NY 10010

www.continuumbooks.com

First published 1978
This edition first published 2005

British Library Cataloguing-in-Publication Data
A catalogue record for this book is available from the British Library.

ISBN 0-8264-7967-7
Designed and typeset by Benn Linfield
Photographic images by Nick Shah and Louise Dugdale
Printed and bound in the United Kingdom by Cromwell Press, Wiltshire

Acknowledgments

The publishers are grateful to Archie Hill and Mary Craig for giving permission to print extracts from their separate articles published in *The Listener*, to *The Times* for allowing the publication of part of an article by Brian Silcock, and to the University of Oklahoma Press for permission to quote from 'The Sacred Pipe'. Continuum regret any unwitting infringement of copyright and would request that any such copyright owner contact them.

Contents

Ikons, Idols, Images

East by West

Puritans & Players

I met Sydney Carter in the last years of his life. I met him in and through his hymns and songs.

Some years ago, I started to organise a Jewish Friday evening meal in a Church Hall I rented in the Portobello Road. It was open to all and people were encouraged to bring wine and food with them. Portobello Road is bedsit territory in London and the evenings were well attended. A Jewish Lord dropped in, as did an Evangelical Choir and students on a pub crawl.

So I needed to find a form of Jewish liturgy which would be effective and inclusive for all the people who turned up. Sydney Carter's hymns and songs were just what we needed. Hymns like 'One More Step Along the World I go' reflected the reality of the world which we all faced.

Carter was a Quaker. Many Jewish people are strongly attracted to Quaker spirituality. I was one of them. What was attractive was a straightforward relationship with God, unencumbered by history, communalism or ritual. This was exactly the appeal of Sydney's hymns and songs, and their impact on our Friday evening assemblies was profound.

These were tunes that anyone could hum and sing — the 'Lord of the Dance' (without the reference to the Pharisees) is perhaps the most celebrated of all — but they spoke directly to the human condition without fuss and with honesty.

We all felt at home with Sydney's religion, the religion exemplified in his hymns.

This religion was relevant to life as it was and not as we should like it to be.

We could recognise our own lives in the lyrics.

The songs started out from exactly where people found themselves to be. They were non-judgemental, welcoming and upbeat. They did not leave you with emotion that you did not know how to use and this emotion was channelled into charity.

Carter was not trying to sell you anything nor was he presupposing anything. His song was your song.

Sydney Carter was a loner. He 'dropped in' on other religious traditions. He did not feel he had to belong. If Jesus or God lived in you, that was enough. He respected people's individuality.

To my mind, he was Britain's greatest hymn-writer of the twentieth century. Just as Percy French had created the folk song of Modern Ireland, so Carter created the hymn of modern people. His songs gave you courage on the way to the dentist, or on the way to visit the accountant or the bank manager.

In the last years of his life Carter was afflicted by Alzheimer's disease and was hospitalised. Increasingly he failed to recognise his family and close friends. But he invariably responded to a visitor singing one of his hymns. Through his own darkness he could still recognise the spark of his own spiritual creativity. It was moving to witness.

Rock of Doubt is what I would term one of the 'humble classics' of English life. Into this same category I would put Isaak Walton's *Compleat Angler* or Wainwright's magnificent guides to fell walking. These are accounts of doing simple things but profound ones.

These authors never set out to make a mark, to be successful or to become idols.

But this was their success.

Lionel Blue
February 2005

The other book

This is the exploded ruin of a book I failed to write. A cool, critical, objective survey of current experiments in Christian worship: that is what I had in mind. To do this, I got a grant from the Joseph Rowntree Charitable Trust. In two years time, I told them, they would have the typescript.

That was seven years ago. How could I have been so lacking in self-knowledge? I had pictured myself, I suppose, as a kind of scientist directing, from the outside, an experiment. I failed to see that I myself would be cooking in the crucible.

Once I began to ask what it was that Christians had to communicate and whether it was true or not, I was in trouble. That is when the book blew up, and questions that I had dreaded now came flying through the air. What did I really think of Jesus as compared to the Buddha, Socrates or even his own follower, St Francis of Assisi? Did I really believe in him or not? What exactly did 'believe in' really mean? Did I really 'believe in' anything at all? Was my haunted feeling that I had to end up a believer based on nothing but panic?

To face such questions had become more urgent than to weigh the pros and cons of rocking the liturgy or dancing half naked in Liverpool Cathedral. My health, my sanity, my wholeness depended on it. If I could not dare to trust the truth—about Jesus, about myself, about anything whatever—then what in the whole creation was it possible to trust? Loyalty to truth came before loyalty to Christianity.

As I dug into the roots of my dubious belief and steeled myself to declare (if the truth should demand it) that I was an atheist I gave a thought, from time to time, to the Joseph Rowntree Charitable Trust. Should I give them back the money which they had advanced? The question was academic, for the money had been spent. Their attitude was Quakerly. Trust the truth (they told me in effect) and keep on digging.

Whether what I have turned up will be of use to anybody but myself I do not know: but here it is.

by christ of any other
name the truth would
always be
the same

Ikons
Idols
Images

The Question? Mark

1

Over every statement, never mind who makes it, there will hang a question mark. *Is this statement true or not?* That is what it will be saying.

Over any statement in these pages, including those which are quoted, whether from Black Elk or the New Testament, look out for that question mark.

It has taken me seven years to write this book. Now, at last, I can see what it was really about. It was about that question mark which first I feared, but later came to celebrate. Without that question mark, I see, there could be no faith or doubt, nothing but dead certainty. Just as there can be no courage without danger, so there can be no faith without uncertainty. Risk is part of the game that we are born to play in. We must learn to lean on possibilities.

So, I dare to play; to try first one thing, then another. These chapters, these quotations, are like the actors on a stage. Let them contradict each other. They are not there to *tell* the truth but to provoke it, to discover it: to start it from the thicket.

The pagans are wrong and The Christians are right!

✝ Chanson de Roland

14

HOPE
+
FEAR

2

Fear lies at the root of all religion: fear of God, fear of the Devil or (to put it un-theologically) fear about the way things are. Rightly so: there is a lot to be afraid of. But there is something else: a defiant, dancing hope that dares to leap and celebrate in the face of all things that would crucify it.

'Crucify': a Christian word. If I were a Buddhist, I might use another. For a Christian, this hope will be incarnate in the shape of Jesus. Am I a Christian? Yes and no. Am I a Buddhist? Yes and no. Forget about the labels; find out what is in the bottle. What is there, in Christianity, for me?

I am haunted, tempted and invited by a Jesus who may or may not be the Jesus of the churches. Not a God who once, and once. alone, put on a human body. That kind of God does not seem probable to me. Either we are all the embodiment of our creator–some in ways that are strange and terrible–or none is. Out of what could the world be made, if not himself? But Jesus, I am ready to admit, is an embodiment which encourages our hope. If reality can wear a form like this, then reality is better than we had supposed.

I am not helped by the miracles attributed to Jesus: Virgin birth, walking on the water, or appearing to disciples after he was dead. These things may have happened, exactly as the Bible says; they may not have happened. There is no sci-entific way to settle it. So I cannot positively disbelieve; but my lack of disbelief could not be described as Faith. It is not a thing that I can lean upon in time of trouble.

All I can lean upon is the challenge I receive from this man who dared to call himself the son of God, dared to say that sins were forgiven, dared to say that we must love our enemies, dared to say (as if he'd seen it happening already) that the poor were lucky and the mourners comforted and, most daringly of all, hailed his own creator as lovable and to be trusted. All these things are what we hope for; Jesus says that we shall have them. He lived and died as if there could be no doubt about it.

Jesus, you might almost say, created the image of a lovable creator in the way that Shakespeare created *Hamlet* and Michelangelo his David. None of these acts of creation would be possible unless reality contained the possibility they realised. You could put it in another way: you could say that Jesus, Michelangelo and Shakespeare were the vehicles of revelation. Jesus, you could say, revealed the lovability of God, the forgivability of sin, the reversability of all our shame and sorrow. This hope, this inherent possibility, found a living image in the life of Jesus.

Is it a convincing image? You could ask that question of the work of Bach, or Mozart. It convinces those equipped with the sensitivity to be convinced. Beauty cannot touch you unless you have a sense of beauty. Music is meaningless if you are deaf. To respond to any revelation of this kind you must have the sensitivity of faith.

Faith is not the same thing as belief. 'The devils also believe', said Jesus 'and they tremble'. What the devils lack is faith. Faith, like love, is higher than belief or disbelief: it is a response provoked, awakened, in the looker or the listener. Even if it could be proved (which is impossible) that the Gospels were fictitious, they could still provoke our faith, like the fictions of a Shakespeare or Cervantes.

I believe that Jesus, unlike Don Quixote, was a man who actually lived. How far the picture which we get from the Bible is 'true', I cannot say. Each one of us, in a sense, must make a Jesus for himself. By accepting or rejecting what the Gospel writers wrote, by interpreting this way or that, each of us must make a choice. This is unavoidable.

So, I choose my Jesus. I have faith in, I am sensitive to, this or that part of the revelation which I find through Jesus. My Jesus is surrounded by a question mark. Lack of conclusive proof concerning what he said or did is an essential element of what he is. What kind of proof can I expect?

Round the lips of pre-classical, archaic statues of the Gods and Goddesses of ancient Greece hovers a playful smile: iron-ical and yet serene. There, I find an answer to my question.

'The question you ask is not the right one. The proof you seek is not the kind of proof that matters. Back your hunch and take your chances: that is how the game is played. You are part of the creation, so create. To create, you have to play. You ask for dead certainties; all we offer is a living possibility. Sulk, and you will get no pity. So take up your fate, your cross (if you prefer to call it that) and use it to create'.

The Jesus that I choose is one who takes up the challenge of the gods and goddesses. 'You are right', he says 'that is how the game is played. So, I create. I show the song I hear, the dance I feel. This is what I choose, and I back it with my life'.

this
is
my
body

the
holy
bread
the
holy
wine
the
holy
pipe

We have been told that Jesus Christ was crucified, but that he shall come again at the Last Judgement, the end of this world or cycle. This I understand and know that it is true, but the white man should know that for the red people too it was the will of the Wakan Tanka, the Great Spirit, that an animal turn itself into a two-legged person in order to bring the most holy pipe; and we too were taught that this white Buffalo Cow Woman, who brought our sacred pipe, will appear again at the end of this 'world', a coming which we Indians know is not very far off.

BLACK ELK of the Ogala Sioux
recorded and edited by Joseph Epes Brown
THE SACRED PIPE, Penguin

How Sweet the Name

3

I have a block about the name of Jesus.

I have been morally blackmailed by the name of Jesus for as long now as I can remember. Uttered in a certain tone of voice, it forbade rational investigation. It set up a warning buzz which paralysed sincerity. It was like the word 'sex' in reverse. Sex said 'You musn't', Jesus said 'You must'.

Must what? Believe that Jesus was the son of God (whatever that could mean), did things that were impossible (like rising from the dead), was deeply grieved by the wicked things I did, yet forgave me if I could believe all this.

Gentle Jesus loved you in an awful way: inside this velvet glove there was a fist of iron. For if you could not believe, you went to hell. Paradoxically, I could believe in hell more than I could in Jesus. To be exact, I could believe in horror. Horror was a first-hand experience; Jesus was only hearsay. Snakes, skeletons, a visit to the dentist showed me hell. Even the thought of everlastingness—in heaven even, let alone in hell—filled me with a giddy dread. On top of that there was the thought of the people I would disappoint if I could not believe in Jesus—of the shocked and stricken looks that I would get. To say that I did not love Jesus would be like uttering the worst four letter word I could imagine. I would condemn myself to exile from the world of sane and loving people. I would show my leprosy.

So it was necessary to believe. But how? How can you believe what is unbelievable? How could I love this sweetly smiling, suffering and sexless Jesus who had put me in this impossible position?

JESUS for me was the supreme example of what Gregory Bateson calls 'the double bind'. I was ordered to do two things which were mutually impossible—to be sincere, and to believe—and, at the same time, forbidden to declare the fact. Jesus, gentle Jesus, was the great forbidder. In his name I was prohibited from being all I really was; and what made it doubly disgusting was the way people went on about Jesus —how wonderful he was, how lucky for us that he had been born, etc.

Frankly, I wished he never had been born. Things were bad enough without Jesus telling me to stand upon my head and pretend (quite sincerely) that it was the right way up.

It was not fair; but you were not allowed to say it. Was I the only one, I wondered, who saw, or thought he saw, the Emperor was naked? I felt in the same predicament as a friend of mine who, as a child, was sitting in his father's car as they drove along a road in Sussex. Suddenly, against the Downs, he saw the outline of a tall, white, faceless figure: the Long Man of Wilmington. For years afterwards, he never said a word about it, for he thought that nobody could see it but himself.

That is how I felt about Jesus. I was in a minority of one: a cuckoo in the holy nest. Maybe, when I grew up, I would learn how to believe like other people. The alternative was too bad to contemplate. Round the name of Jesus was a threatening and fragrant hush. It was like the smell of lilies at a funeral. Sometimes when I go to church, I catch it still, and I feel my stomach rising.

I have to make an effort of will to look beyond the name of Jesus to the man behind it. To rcsurrect him from this sweetly stinking sepulchre, I have to hold my breath, and shut my eyes.

What is folk is never fixed or final

The Jesus Ballad

even though you write it down, it

Looking for what Jesus actually said and did is like looking for the original version of an ancient ballad. The four Gospels are like four variants. By the time they started to be written down the folk process had already got to work. You cannot keep a live tradition down: it will go on sprouting new interpretations. If you do not like them, you can call them heresies. But any singer worth the name, will keep on reaching for the song behind the song. You can call that going back, or going forward. To interpret you must recreate.

Though authority may tell you otherwise, there is nothing fixed or final in a live tradition. Petrify it and you kill it. Bibles, churches, song books too, are the servants of tradition. If they try to be its master, they become its undertaker.

With songs, a distinction can be drawn between those which have a known composer and are published in a version which can be fairly called 'correct', and those which are of unknown origin. No one can say for sure whether the latter are 'correct' or not or whether they are the work of a single author and composer or of many. Folk songs fall into the second category. So does Christianity.

Besides the four Gospels which are in the Bible there were other gospels, called Apochryphal, which the editors rejected as corrupted, 'incorrect'. But we cannot be sure that their own versions were 'correct'. The whole notion of 'correctness' may, as in folk song, be a phantom anyway.

Those who believe that the Gospel writers (unlike others) were divinely prevented from ever making a mistake, will reject the folk analogy. I can only say that I do not believe what they believe; furthermore, I cannot see why anybody should, unless they are so obsessed by the thirst for infallibility that they cannot face the facts of life. God, or providence, or whatever other name you like to give to the source of our reality, does not seem to work the way they think.

If Providence was so anxious to provide us with certainties, it might at least have arranged that Jesus should leave us a signed statement on some of the questions which so divide us: such as:

Must a Christian be a pacifist? Is divorce ever permissible? And (if not) what exactly constitutes a marriage?

The function of the Bible, like the function of the world itself is not to provide us with security, but to force us to create. Faith is the faculty which makes creation possible. 'Christian' faith is just a particular way of using a gift which we make use of every minute of our lives, consciously or otherwise. By faith we travel from what is to what we hope for. Faith, as St. Paul says, is the evidence of things not seen; things which do not exist in time and space but which, by our labour, can be given an expression in time and space. All arts, from painting to agriculture, are made possible by faith.

Faith cannot feed on infallibility: there has to be an element of risk. To put one foot in front of another, I must exercise my faith, and take a chance, however minimal. As a device for forcing us to exercise faith on a heroic scale, Christianity could hardly be improved on. By Christianity I mean the whole perplexing, exasperating, mind blowing apparatus by which the messages of Jesus have been handed down. It dangles before us, not a saving certainty, but a bright, blurred possibility that fills the heart with hope and discontent and dares us to make the necessary leap. Christianity kindles the imagination; through all the broken and corrupted variants we catch the echo of the song behind the song. Does it come to us from the past or from the future? We can never know. The Gospels, the written records, play their part; but they cannot give us the kind of certainty we look for. Christianity is incurably folk: it forces us to recreate it. If we cannot, it will die.

Keeps on growing

The Present Tense

A revelation ought to be so clear that you cannot deny it. The sun is such a revelation. The fact that we live is such a revelation. Pain is such a revelation; so is beauty.

These revelations do not come by hearsay. If you had only read about them in a book there would be no compelling reason to believe that they were true. A book can lie.

The Christian revelation concerning the nature of reality and what we need to do about it came through Jesus. What Jesus said and did is told in the New Testament. Some of the events reported are not easy to believe. How can we check whether they are true or not? We can't. They happened, or did not happen, nineteen hundred years ago.

Unless we can meet the Christian revelation here and now, it is not a revelation. It cannot compel belief. All the New Testament can do is to point to something which is still available.

If, for example, there is someone living here and now who can show, in his or her life and words, what Jesus showed, the revelation may convince. Is there such a person?

Again, the Gospel story itself, whether historically true or false, may still compel by what, for want of a better word or image, I will call its beauty. It may awaken hope or love.

Not by historical evidence, which can never be conclusive, but only by provoking our imagination, by raising up the life inside us: only by showing us something which was already there, though we may not have noticed it before, can the Gospel lead us to this kind of revelation.

So what it comes to in the end is this: dare we trust the revelation which the Gospel calls up from the depths of our own reality? Dare we trust they possibility it offers? If we can, does it matter how we came to do it? The Gospel story, whether historically true or not, could still be regarded as a parable: that is, as a working model, cast in fictitious form, of the way things really are.

Can we accept the truth of a parable without accepting it as literally true? Of course. How else could we accept the truth in the parables of Jesus?

The truth of parable is timeless. The truth of history is the truth about particular events in the present or the past. Once past, there is no way to prove, beyond all doubt, that they actually happened. All that can be established is a probability.

The only truth which we can trust is the truth which is in the present tense. Only the truth of parable, because it is beyond all time, can speak to us for ever in the present tense.

Parable and history may coincide: a story which is historically true may also present us with the truth of parable. The Gospel story may be historically accurate. But even if it is, it is by the truth of the parable, not by the truth of history, that we are healed.

A man is drowning: a rope comes spinning down, he clutches it, and he is saved. Who wove this rope, this parable? Some say Peter, some say Paul. But to the drowning man the important question is: will it bear my weight or not?

Who wove the rope is a question about history. You may get it wrong and still be saved.

There is no saving revelation, then, except this revelation in the present tense. What happened in Palestine nineteen hundred years ago may have started the chain of events leading to the revelation we receive today. Gospels, creeds, works of art, ritual and above all, the lives of countless men and women may have conducted it, as a wire conducts electricity; as the human body, through the act of reproduction, transmits life through centuries and centuries. But it is the shock which hits us here and now, the living body that we see today, that is the effective revelation. All that records of the past can do for us, all that legend, fairy tale or works of art can do for us, all that living Christians (or non-Christians) can do for us, is to raise in each of us the question that Jesus raised in the disciples: is this a possibility we dare to trust?

The living Jesus is this possibility. You do not have to call it Jesus. You need not know, or believe, that Jesus ever lived.

The function of the church is not to rush round getting pagans, Jews, Buddhists or anyone to sign a legal document saying 'I believe there was a man called Jesus, and He was the Son of God'. The function of the Church is to embody the hope, the danger, the beauty and the possibility held out by Jesus (if he lived: or by some incredible fiction writers if he didn't). Whether he did or didn't doesn't matter any more. If all the Bibles were destroyed, if the name of Jesus were forgotten, it wouldn't matter any more so long as the fire kindled–the hope, the beauty, the possibility–still went on burning. Would Jesus care if we forgot him? Is he so anxious to keep his copyright?

GOD in trouble

is ~~safe~~ at risk

If God is perfect and omnipotent, how can He possibly be in trouble? But He is. God is angry, even jealous, in the Old Testament. He is crucified in the New Testament. Omnipotent or not, He is in trouble.

Who made the trouble? Man, or the Devil? But who made man and the Devil? God: Deny it, and you are a dualist, a heretic.

'He gave man liberty, which he misused'. God must have known the possibility: He made trouble for Himself. Why? He didn't have to. So, He must have wanted it: the possibility of trouble anyway.

Was God so bored with his perfect equanimity that He had to set Himself a puzzle, put Himself at risk? It seems childish to suggest it. But what else can you suggest? And if God was bored, He was already in trouble: before the fall of man, or the fall of Lucifer. There was a worm in the apple from the very start. Who could have put it there, but God?

So (to put it crudely) there is something lacking: an inbuilt incompleteness in the very nature of reality. Why create if you have all you want already? God needed something; so, he had to make it. Hence, creation.

It is a mystery: but here we are, in the middle of the mystery, and we have to nibble at it, try to make some kind of sense of it. Why? It is our nature to. We have to make order or meaning: or discover it.

'God created man in His own image' and man is certainly in trouble. Is that because God must be in trouble too: that there is a certain bias—a restlessness, a risk, an unpredictability, a danger even, in the very nature of reality? That the Fall is not an accident—how could it be an 'accident', anyway, if God is outside time and therefore knows the future as well as the present and the past?

If not an accident, the Fall is a part of the way things were from the beginning: or (if you prefer) the way things are.

What, then, of the perfection and omnipotence of God? His perfection and omnipotence must include what seems to us the very opposite: His incompleteness, His vulnerability. In which case, Jesus is the very image of divinity in a way that we could hardly dare to think.

We could not dare to think it, because it is so unsettling: it strikes at the heart of all our wishful thinking, all our longing for eternal rest. We may want it (apparently) but God does not. God *needs* trouble. All we can hope for is to see it as God sees it: to travel with the Creator in whose image we are so uncomfortably made.

?

Unless the game
was rigged from
the beginning
then the FALL
suggests that
LUCK not
GOD is Lord of
All

7

Shut the Bible up. But then open it again. Do not use it in the way you did before. Do not use it as a bludgeon. Do not say I must believe it because it is the Word of God. It is not the word of God (the Quakers said this long ago) any more than a chair or table, or Shakespeare or Hamlet, is the word of God. (The Quakers did not say that: I did.) The word of God is in the Bible, said George Fox; but the word of God is in you and me as well. The word in the Bible and the word in me must spark and kindle like a flash of lightning.

The Bible is a precious book. But you can make an idol of it. You can make an idol out of anything, however good. You can make an idol out of God, or Jesus. You can make an idol out of Shakespeare or Karl Marx. And, as Zen Buddhists are well aware, you can make an idol of the Buddha. 'Walk in the Way. If the image of the Buddha rises up to block it, kill the Buddha'.

Ikons, idols, images are necessary; but you have to use them in the proper way. They are fingers pointing (Zen again). The Bible is a forestful of fingers pointing. Worship what they point to, not the fingers.

What is the proper way to use the Bible? I regard it as a big *koan*, not as a record of historical events. Even though it is a book of historical events, even though the events recorded may be true. How can we know if they are true or not? All we can ever say is that they are probable. What we are saved by, healed by, is the timeless truth of parable. Truth that is historical may contain a parable. I do not doubt myself that there was an actual Jesus; that the things he is reported to have said and done are based on fact. Whether they were rightly reported or interpreted I do not know.

without the Christ within the Christ of history would be no use to us at all

To the Truth

8

Truth is to be trusted.

To trust it is an act of faith.

Any statement of the truth is to be tested.

To test it is an act of doubt.

Faith and doubt both serve the truth.

To crush either by an act of terror, in another or oneself, does no service to the truth.

I may be wrong; but honesty in being wrong will be rewarded.

If it isn't, I was wrong to trust the truth.

The Ikon of Mary

For most of my life now I have kept a Russian ikon which I cut out from *Lilliput*. It is a paper reproduction; but an ikon, whether reproduced or painted on a piece of wood, it is still an ikon. Formal, almost diagrammatic, it expresses the relationship between the Holy Child and Mother. She is supporting him, yet he is supporting her. By his very need of her, he brings to birth that love, and strength, and courage which she might not have without. That, at any rate, is what it says to me: that we are supported, not only by the strength of our creator, but by his weakness too. By the love and compassion which it kindles in us, we are made heroic; which I would like to be, but seldom am. By this ikon I remember how it can be made to happen.

This Christian mandala of the Mother and the Child is more compelling than a picture of the Holy Trinity. The Trinity may speak to the intellect, but this duality speaks to an emotion too. It is hard to imagine what a Trinity would look like but we have no difficulty with a mother and a child. The image is so powerful that, to a Protestant, it verges on the dangerous. Christ may be depicted as divine: but to give his mother equal billing, as it were, in a statue or a picture, might suggest that she is nearly God as well. And so, in most of our old English churches the images of the Holy Mother have been smashed.

Neither Catholic nor Orthodox would dare to claim that she is God. She might reflect the Holy Light; but she is not, like Christ, the untreated Light itself. That is the theory. In practice, many see God better in the mirror when they try to look at God directly as the Father or the Son.

One who is neither Catholic nor Protestant might ask: how exactly, can we look at God, excepting in a mirror? In any case, he might argue, light is light, whichever way it reaches us; and light reflected in a concave mirror can be brighter, hotter, and more concentrated than the light which comes directly from the sun. What about a Laser beam?

Since we cannot look at either Jesus or his mother now—only their contemporaries could do that—all the light that we receive is reflected or refracted. So any image which can focus or collect that light should be gratefully received and venerated; which the image of the Holy Mother is, by Catholic and Orthodox.

A mythologist might argue that the cult of Mary owes as much to pagan as to Christian sources; that the worship paid to her is a carry over of the worship that was paid to Isis or Diana or to that Great Mother whose strange ikons have come down to us from Neolithic times. He might claim that Jesus too is the inheritor of all the dying, resurrected Gods that came before—of Mithras, of Adonis, even Odin. This is probably true; and what else would you expect? If Christ, as Christians claim, is the fulfiller of all human hope, all non-Christian religions would have to be the non-Jewish equivalent of the Old Testament, which would lend some of its colour, some of its practices and imagery, to the New.

The cult of Mary seems to answer a need, felt by men as well as women, for an ikon which could render justice to the female side of the Creator. All the Hindu gods have their female counterpart. To the Catholic, one might almost dare to say—to the emotional if not the intellectual part—Mary is the feminine of Jesus. By their works ye shall know them, not by their theology; and their works would include their works of art.

The figure of Mary, *Stella Maris*, shining like a star or lighthouse over the dark and stormy ocean that we navigate, would present no problem to a Jungian. She has risen from the depths of Man's unconscious awareness of the way things are, like Aphrodite from the sea. There just had to be a Mary, whether you called her by that name or something else; just as there had to be some kind of Jesus, too. The fact that both Jesus and Mary were historical, that they actually lived in time is not the real reason, or not the only one, why they are worshipped and remembered still. Unless the historical had coincided with a psychological and spiritual necessity they would not have left a mark; we should have forgotten them. The Christ within is brought to birth and corroborated by the Christ without—the Christ that we encounter in the Gospels, the traditions and the ikons of the Church. But the reverse is also true; they are corroborated by the Christ within, the ikon of reality which we carry in our bones. Unconsciously, it may be. Prophetically.

So it may be with Mary, too; and if it is, we have not seen the last of her. Even the Protestant may need that ikon after all.

Whenever

2 or 3

10

'Whenever two or three are gathered together in my name, there am I in the midst of you'. The kingdom of heaven is within: but you cannot get it out, excepting with the help of other people. By their otherness you dig to what is in yourself.

Not only the kingdom of heaven is within, but the kingdom of hell. Whenever 2 or 3 are gathered together in the name of anything–God, the Devil, Newcastle United–something is liberated. Not only a Quaker meeting but a lynching mob provides strong evidence of this.

So, we need our friends. One friend is enough to start with. By my neighbour or my wife, by my cat or toad or dog, even, I unlock what I carry in myself. Books, songs, pictures, trees are friends; I must choose them carefully, or I may unlock what is better left locked up. I carry for them, they carry for me, the keys of heaven and of hell.

If I encounter Jesus–in the Gospels, in the life or conversation of a friend–the Jesus that I carry in myself is called to life. 'The Scriptures are not the Word of God' as George Fox said 'But the Word of God is in the Scriptures'. The Word of God is in George Fox, and me, as well. From the Word encountered in the Scriptures to the Word in me, there flies a spark, igniting what I carry.

So, the Church. The Church is the community, by which I find myself: or that portion of myself which I wish to find by our dedication to a common purpose. By words and music, or by silence: by processing, kneeling or by being still, we call up, by our common effort, what is lurking in the dark of each and all of us.

Love your neighbour as yourself: for yourself is in your neighbour. You can only find it through your neighbour. Do not think about God, for the moment: think about your deepest self, the self that you can only find by being with somebody else. That body does not have to be a human body: it may be the body of an animal, a piece of sculpture, or a star ten million miles away. It need not be tangible: it may take the form of a body made by sound, as in music, or a structure made of words. It may even seem to take the form of your own body, as in running, jumping, dancing, riding on a surf board or a horse. There is a kind of otherness in your own body; what comes from deep inside you might as well be coming from outside you. From deep inside you or from deep outside you, you come into contact with an otherness which is, yet is not, yourself.

Words collapse in face of this experience: all they can do is to point towards it. Self and not-self intermingle all the time. You are your own neighbour, and your neighbour you. Love is where you feel, most sharply, the absurdity, the falsity of your position as a separated being. Yet, by this very separation, this absurdity, you are able to express what you could not express in any other way. By your very otherness, you are able to celebrate identity.

Now, think of God: that 'altogether otherness' of the Moslem and the Jew. Is not this very otherness a part of what you are: is it not necessary to define you?

As the male defines the female, and the dark the light, so the otherness of God defines my own identity. You cannot have the One, without the Other. You cannot have the I, without the You.

So whether you abase yourself before the Otherness of God, or glory (like the Hindu in your Oneness with God, you are only using a special or a verbal image to point to what cannot be said. The self is a paradox: you can only find it when you lose it. Which is what Jesus (very nearly) said. 'You must lose your life to find it'. What is your life, if not yourself? And where can you find it, except by the otherness of the neighbour or of God: except by that Otherness which you carry in yourself? What pronoun will you pin it down by: how are you to address this otherness? 'I? You? He? She? It? We? They? You could make a case for any, or all of them. For, as the Vedas say, 'Tat Tvam Asi'– I am that. Grammar gives up. Language expires, in the attempt to say it: and, by its very death, does point at last to what it cannot say.

Imitation noitatiml of to Christ tzinnᗡ

For I believed then
and I believe now
that God — as
part of I know not
what inscrutable
purpose —
allowed them
to believe they
were unbelievers.
And that at the
moment of their
passing, perhaps
the blindfold
was removed.

from
SAINT
EMMANUEL
THE
GOOD
MARTYR.

by
Miguel
de
Unamuno

Can Christ really be imitated? Yes and no.

Pacifists often ask: 'Can you imagine Jesus with a gun?' No, I can't; but it does not follow that I must be a pacifist. I cannot imagine Jesus as a father, still less as a mother. That does not mean that procreation has to stop.

Some Christians, it is true, have taken the view that procreation ought to stop.

St Paul seems to have thought that marriage was a second best: 'It is better to marry than to burn'. It would be hard to deny in Christian tradition (but not in Jewish) a lurking prejudice in favour of virginity. The fact that Jesus was not married (or, if he was, that we have no record of it) has a lot to do with this.

Jesus was not an actor or a miner. If we try to do what Jesus did and nothing else, we find ourselves in an impossible position. Jesus never wrote a book; so, there ought to be no Gospel. No Christian, I feel, would go that far. So, where do we draw the line?

Carl Gustav Jung claimed to be a Christian. Many Christians would disallow the claim, but I think that Jung was right about imitating Jesus. He said (I quote from memory of what his secretary said, upon a T.V. programme): 'We must imitate Jesus only in following, as faithfully as Jesus did, whatever may be true for us'.

That, God knows, would be difficult enough. But it allows for a different vocation for each human being. He (or she) is not condemned to try, impossibly, to be a carbon copy of the Jesus who lived in Palestine.

So, it may be right for me to be a pacifist; but not because Jesus never held a gun. Or even a sword. Or it may be right (as Colin Morris thinks) for an African Christian to engage in armed revolt or sabotage. Each must act according to the time and place, the age and sex: according to his peculiar ability, or even disability (such as having to live in an iron lung, or being an epileptic, or a schizophrenic). Vocation comes by disability, as well as ability. Whatever cup our life may come in, we must drink it. 'Take up your cross and follow me': said Jesus: but our cross may be a very different shape from his.

We must be as open as Jesus was to the leading of what he called 'The Father'; though we may be led to address it by another name. We may be called to orthodoxy, or to protest. We may be called to question the authority of Church or Bible; though we cannot expect the Church, or the Bible worshippers, to see that our vocation is a valid one. We may be mistaken. That, in itself, may be the cross that we are called to bear: to be honestly mistaken, to maintain a position which will be shown, in the end, to be untenable.

WHY DO YOU CALL ME GOOD?

NO ONE IS GOOD BUT GOD

Jesus

goodbye
Jesus

12

The further you go from Him, the nearer you get to Him.

You say goodbye to one Jesus: to the God who once and once alone walked in a human body.

What is left? Only a man; unique, as all men are, yet typical. All that he can do a man can do. Whether he has or hasn't is another matter.

What is he doing? Calling you to liberty, to the breaking of all idols that would cower you, including the idol which he has become himself.

Including the idols of joy and sorrow. Blessed are they that mourn, he says, for they shall be comforted.

Including the idols of power and precedence. The first shall be last, he says; the last first.

Including the idols of God. No man has seen God at any time; yet, if you have seen me, you have seen the father.

Including the idol of safety: save your life, and you will lose it.

And yet they have made another idol out of him, bedangled him with miracles. Blaspheme against this idol, and (they say) you go to hell.

To find him, you must leave him. Turn your back upon the idol: a strangely seductive idol yet, ultimately, unbelievable. There is something false about that sweet and gentle smile. That crown of thorns has become a diadem, made of real gold and jewels. That invitation to be free has become an imperial command. That manger has become a sepulchre. The Holy Image has become an Iron Maiden: inside it, Jesus, trying to get out.

Say goodbye to the official Jesus. Talk about it to the man beside you, walking to Emmaus. He is anonymous. If he is God, then so are you.

Bibles, legends, history are signposts: they are pointing to the future, not the past. Do not embrace the past or it will turn into an idol.

But where are you living, Jesus, now you're dead? *I'm living where I always did, he said. Cleave the wood and you will find me, strike the stone and I am there.*

Zen Jesus

13

Love your enemies: for you and they are opposite ends of the same thing. Both are necessary, like the hero and the villain in the play. The only thing that is real is the play itself.

Your sins are forgiven: that is to say, you are reunited with the whole of which you are a part, as soon as you see what is really happening. When you do, you will forgive others. If you can't, it's an indication that you haven't really seen the way things are.

My yoke is easy and my burden light. Do not be too anxious about tomorrow. Once you no longer identify so painfully with your 'individual' self, a great load will be taken off your back. Even death will not worry you so much. The sting of death is sin, i.e. a wrong view of the way things are, which fills you with panic, meanness and forboding.

Let go of what you never really 'have'—possessions, security, position, etc.: you'll feel much better. Travel with the truth of what you really are and then, though poor, you will inherit the earth. It's all yours, it always has been, as far as anything can belong to anybody.

You want to see the truth: well, I am it. You won't see any other kind. You want me to show you God: I do. Look at what I am, and do: there is no other way for me to show it. I am a man, yet I am the Son of God: so are you. All you have to do is realise it. Once you do, then all I do you will be able to.

Are you worried, because I have to leave you? I die: but I am with you always. This bread is my body, this wine my blood. Whenever two or three are gathered together with me in mind, I am there. You believe me because you've seen me? Some are lucky: they can do it without.

way out | way in

East
by
West

EAST by WEST

14

There are two ways to get to China: you can travel east or travel west. The usual way to get there from Europe was to travel east. But Columbus, believing that the world was global, went the other way. He never reached Japan or China; he thought, mistakenly, that he had reached India. He had in fact done something quite unexpected: discovered America. It was left for Magellan to circumnavigate the globe and prove that Columbus had been right. You could go east by going west.

For China, read the Christian Faith: there are two ways of getting to it. You can follow the accustomed route, with its many different branches, Orthodox, Catholic or Protestant. Or you can turn your back on it and sail off in the opposite direction in the hope that we are living on a globe and that truth can still be found by sailing either east or west. On the way you may find something you did not expect (America) but if you plug on faithfully you'll get to China in the end. That at any rate is what I hope for.

But why bother, when there is a shorter way? For the same reason that Columbus had to bother. What had been the easier route was easier no longer. Turks and Tartars barred the way. If you couldn't get to China now by sailing away from it (which to many seemed impossible) then it was goodbye to China; for the moment anyway.

For most non-Christians in what used to be called Christendom there are two main obstacles to Christian belief. One is the idea —not so much an idea, as a climate of opinion—to the effect that there is no God anyway, so all religion is a waste of time. The other is the blinkered, flat-earth point of view of most Christian believers: they believe that there is only one way to China and only one word to describe it: 'China'.

Christianity is based on a series of historical or allegedly historical events. In that, Christianity is not unique; many religions, Buddhism included, claim that certain things occurred at a particular time and place. For the Buddhist, however, it doesn't really matter much whether you can believe that they occurred or not. What matters is whether you are walking in the way indicated by the Buddha; even if you think the story of Buddha and the Bho tree is a fairy tale. For Christians it is different.

Unless you can believe that Jesus actually lived, and did the things which the Bible said he did, you can hardly start to be a Christian at all. You can interpret the miracles 'symbolically', if you like; you can say that the story of Adam, Eve and the Creation is 'poetic'. But there is a limit to all this: usually, it is met when you try to demythologise the Resurrection. Unless Jesus did in fact do what nobody has done before or since, the Christian claim that their revelation is unique falls to the ground. Jesus may have been a holy man who suffered for his virtue; but there have been others. Jesus may have said: 'I am the Way, the Truth, and the Life. No man cometh unto the Father but by me'. But he could have been mistaken; for, after all, he was only human. Had he known more about comparative religion, he might have revised that statement.

To a Fundamentalist, this watering down of dogma is anathema. You must accept the fact (he claims) that God made an incursion into history in a manner which was quite unique: that the Bible is the record of this Incarnation of divinity. You must accept all this or you are not a Christian. Few church attenders are as logical as this: they believe what they can, and hope the rest. But what they must believe, or not be Christian in the accepted sense, is that Jesus was divine and, what is more, uniquely so. Claims on behalf of Mithras, Krishna or any other person, whether historical or merely mythological, must be rejected.

This is what the average non-Christian cannot accept: the Christian claim to a monopoly.

15

I am alive, I shall be dead. I can be sure of nothing else but that.

What being dead may mean, I do not know. I can only see it from the outside: I see other people dying. But to be alive is different: I can see it from the inside.

To be alive is to feel pain and pleasure: to love and fear. To be alive is to be able to create, to think of something which is not and make it happen. How I can do it is a mystery: how I can exist is a mystery.

Every effect must have a cause: that is what we are taught. But I can see no cause for the effect which I am. I wake up, riding on a miracle. All my logic is based upon a solid fact which seems to baffle logicality. Something, apparently, has come of nothing. It is as if my reason is effective on the assumption that the world is flat: and yet, I know the world is round. I live in a paradox.

My reason serves me well. By reasoning I make a road, a chair, a bomb. Yet not by reasoning alone: something leads me on (or pushes me) which I cannot put a name to. My reason is the tool of this. How can I label or describe it?

Desire. Shall I call it that? My desiring is a mystery: how, why, can I do it? Desire is part of the miracle I ride upon: can I say that I do it, or that it is doing me? My desiring is a given thing, like the body I inherit: like this faculty I call my reason, which seems to contradict itself and yet to work.

Consciousness: another mystery. My consciousness is bound up with this body that I live and walk in. I am conscious of the world and of my self. I cannot imagine consciousness before I had a body, or after I am dead. There was no 'I' to be conscious. How did consciousness come out of nothing? What will happen to it when I am no more?

I am impossible; and yet, I am. If that is possible, I see no limit to what may be possible. For practical purposes I think I see a limit: all my reasoning is based on the assumption (which seems to work) that some things are possible and some are not. But I do not really know.

All I know for sure is that I am alive. To be dead, or not yet born, is something I cannot imagine. I do not know what it feels like to be a stone or star: I observe them from the outside, like the fact of being dead or not yet born. All I know for certain, from the inside and the outside (for I can look at my own hand or foot, I can feel the back of my own neck) is the fact that I am living.

This is the only rock that I can build upon.

Baptism of Doubt

16

What we want now is the real baptism. We have been getting our baptism at second hand.

We must go right down into the water, wash our minds of all we ever knew about Christianity. Is this possible? Perhaps not. What we should really wash, perhaps, is not our minds but our hearts; we must get rid of all our false faith, based on fear. We must be ready to believe that all we ever learned in church is nothing but a pack of lies. We must be ready to believe, if truth demands it, that there is no God; that Jesus (if there ever was a Jesus) was an ordinary man who did no miracles and died like anybody else. We must be ready to believe that the Bible, and the Gospels in particular, were written by ordinary men who might have been mistaken. We must credit them with no more authority than the author of the Book of Mormon.

We must put truth first, and not Christianity. If truth leads us to the Gospel of St Matthew (or the Book of Mormon), good. If not, good again. Reality is what we have to look for. There is no other rock to build on. We must trust the truth, for there is nothing else that we can trust.

We must drown our belief in oblivion; then, it may come up again, honest now and innocent. We must become 'like little children'. How are we to do it?

We must trust, first of all, the truth we know already. How can we be certain, absolutely certain, that it is the truth? We can't. That is the very first truth that we must learn to trust: that we cannot be certain. Risk lies at the roof of our reality.

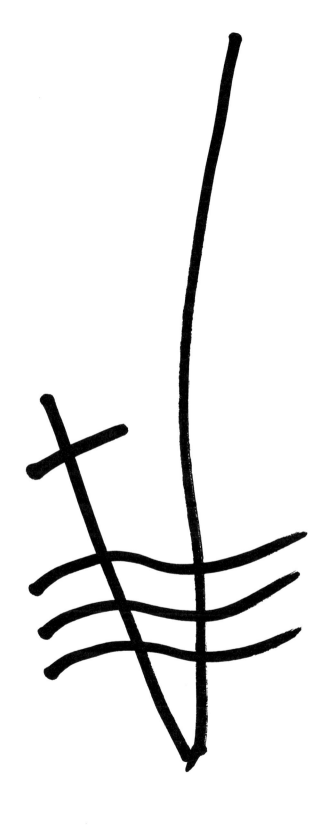

X Y and Z

17

First, I observe the fact that I exist; what next? Material objects: chairs, tables, paper. But the world is not material objects only: there are thoughts, emotions, instincts and the faculty to imagine something and bring it about. These also I observe; though not with the eye or, indeed, with any of the senses.

What about God? I do not observe a God; only the things I have already said. How they came to be and (more urgently) how I came to be myself is a mystery. Whatever creates, upholds and continues to propel them might be described, algebraically, by an X which might be labelled 'God'. I observe, not 'God', but the effects of 'God'.

What I do observe are qualities of kindness, courage, accuracy, beauty which must ultimately be referred, as all things must, to 'God'. The same is true of ugliness and cruelty. I see no reason to suppose that nice things are caused by 'God', and nasty things by something else. I observe things and qualities which conflict with or demolish one another. All of them must come from 'God'.

In the totality of my experience I observe two poles of reality, one of which appears to be good for me, the other not. The same appears to be true for other people and (to some extent) for animals and objects which are inanimate. What destroys an object can hardly be said to be good for it; though if the object does not know what is happening, it cannot be said to suffer in the way a man might suffer.

So I observe what might roughly be described as good and evil. Roughly, because it is not easy to locate them; where they are and what they are will depend on where the observer is. This state of affairs must also be due to 'God'.

I observe, however, that there is a tendency in most religions to equate 'God' with what is good, and to assign what is evil to some other source: to split the basic X into Y and Z. The Y is referred to as 'God' and the Z (sometimes) as 'The Devil'.

I observe (or think I do) that this is an evasion of the facts and is the cause of much confusion. It would be more accurate to speak of the goodness of God and the badness of God. Or

(alternatively) not to refer to the basic X as God at all and rearrange the signs as follows:

$$X = \text{the cause of all there is,}$$
$$Y = \text{the goodness of it,}$$
$$Z = \text{the badness of it.}$$

I observe that the Christians will have none of this. They equate Y with Christ and Christ with X. Z is left out in the cold or 'outer darkness'. Z is regarded as the enemy of X and Y, but how Z came to be is not accounted for.

Logically, this does not add up. But Christians will say that the whole situation is a mystery, beyond all logic; which may well be true. But since, in spite of what they say, the Christians do make use of logic when they speak of God, and Christ, and evil, I think it would be honester if they admitted that (in terms of logic) evil as well as good must come from God. They could still go on supporting Y, and attacking Z. Why should they want to do this? Because X (for reasons known only to itself) seems to have constructed us (including me, and possibly every creature in the world) to want Y to prevail, even though we are partly dominated and confused by Z.

The only logical alternative to this would be to say that reality has two rival sources, Y and Z (God and the Devil). But this the Christians will not allow; this is the heresy of dualism.

I observe (though I cannot account for it) that I feel the Christians are right about this; that reality must have one source. But I see that source as being beyond good and evil, even though it may intend that we should be fighting on the side of good. Why it should intend it is indeed a mystery; but that seems to be the way things are.

Test of Joy

18

If you are unfaithful to your husband or your wife, enjoy it. For unless you do, there is no excuse at all.

To be joyfully good is best. But to be joyfully wicked (if you can) is better than to be miserably good.

'Joyfully wicked': is such a thing possible? Certainly it is possible to enjoy what other people think is wicked. But can you enjoy what you deeply and sincerely feel is wrong? I doubt it. If you can enjoy what you call your wickedness, there must be a part of you which does not really think it wicked. If you hate being 'good', there must be a part of you which does not really think it good.

Is joy, therefore, the only criterion of what is truly bad or good? In a way, I think it is; for joy is not possible without being true to what you really are. If being true to what you really are is wicked, then creation is self contradictory.

Was there joy in Jesus, as he hung upon the cross? Unless he lost faith, I dare to say there was. No pleasure, no enjoyment of the flesh: the agony was real. But if he stayed true to what he really was, his life still pointed homeward, like a needle to the north. There was a kind of joy in that.

If you betray the truth of what you really are, even though the world may call you virtuous, there is a hollow in the heart. Your philanthropy, your laughter and your duty have a maggot in the middle.

'Though I bestow all my goods to feed the poor and though I give my body to be burned, and have not charity, it profiteth me nothing'. So says St Paul. An astonishing statement, which strikes at the root of joyless morality. For you cannot have this thing called charity without a kind of grace or joy. Charity cannot creep: it has to dance or die.

Cardinal Newman (I remember reading somewhere) has not yet been made a saint officially because there is insufficient evidence that he radiated joy. I may have misunderstood or misremembered what I read. But if I did, I think it was an inspired piece of misreading. If Newman was indeed so joyless (I'm not saying that he was) then I think the instinct of the Vatican was right.

I cannot remember the name of the rabbi who declared that at the Final Judgement every man will have to account for all the things he could rightly have enjoyed but didn't. Jesus, I believe, would have approved of this. In the New Testament the Pharisees are the 'good' men who have turned their back to joy; unlike the publicans and sinners. These may not find the joy they seek in what they do; yet, though 'bad', they are facing in the right direction. No wonder Jesus found them more attractive.

A man who knows what joy is, and longs for it, can be more honest with himself than one who doesn't. He may lie to other people; he is less likely to be a liar to himself. If the publican or sinner cannot find the joy he seeks, he knows that he has missed the mark. He can repent; his book-keeping is honest, and tells him where he is in debt. But the Pharisee has fooled himself: he has written down a fortune he does not possess. Discounting the ring of joy, he cannot tell false currency from true. He must drop this phoney load of virtue to get in through the Needle's Eye.

Can it be done? Yes, but the cost is shattering: as Paul discovered. Only an ex-Pharisee, perhaps, could have swung so far in the opposite direction and given us the Thirteenth Chapter of Corinthians.

Living
on
Credit

Who?

19

'You begin by accepting what the churches teach: you structure your life upon it. Hymn books, bells and stained glass windows, the language of the Bible and the liturgy, the language of sermons and theological reviews—you absorb it, almost unconsciously. It is in your bloodstream: it affects the way you think and talk.

Later, you begin to doubt your foundations: the miracles, it may be. But the structure still holds up without foundations, without the scaffolding you have discarded. It is supported by similar structures to the right and left whose foundations may be solider than yours. You have not lost your faith, you say: you believe things in a different way—not literally, but poetically. To those who believe in the firmness of the old foundations, to those of literal and simple faith, you speak in the language they understand. From what you say, they think that your foundations are the same as theirs: you have a mental reservation about this, but feel that your faith is essentially the same as theirs (they might think otherwise).

To those who question the old foundations, you talk another way: about the mythological nature of the Christian story—making it quite clear that what is mythological is not necessarily untrue. A myth can express a truth which cannot be expressed so well another way. 'Why not?' you are asked. You find this difficult to answer.

With either of these two groups you can be quite sincere and honest (well, *essentially* sincere and honest) but when you have to face them both together—in the pulpit, for example—you are in a bit of a fix. Which tongue are you to speak with? You sidestep hell, heaven and creed: you attack on social issues. 'By their fruits ye shall know them' is your text. By their fruits, and not their roots. If the fruits are good, you know the roots are where they should be, even if they are upside down, draining nourishment from hope instead of old fashioned belief, from the present (or the future) rather than the past.

What are your fruits like? In terms of human kindness, in terms of taking up the proper stand on all social issues, not too bad: not worse, anyway, than those of your fundamentalist parishioners.

There is one problem, though: your fruits are no better, maybe not as good, as those who do not claim to be religious at all. Cheerfully atheist, they produce marrows and tomatoes bigger than your own. You find this irritating, but you quell the rebel thought that God is not supporting you the way He should.

God moves in a mysterious way, you say: but cannot avoid the thought that if you had been brought up an atheist you might be doing no worse than you are already, and feel a good deal freer and franker than you are. Speaking with forked tongue to the two halves of your flock, you sometimes feel that God is making you a hypocrite.

Your non-believing co-workers in the fields of philanthropy and politics do not despise you: but they do not envy you. Your Christianity, they feel, is something that you cannot help: like a club foot, or a lisp. It inhibits you: it may even give you a certain old-world charm. It is convenient for them, in that it inhibits you from the more bare-faced forms of rudeness and duplicity. They can make you blush, blackmail you by your Christianity. They may find you lovable, but laughable. Secretly, you rage against all this. You smile joyfully (for a Christian should be joyful), you are gentle and forgiving: but a raven gnaws your liver, and by night your doubts and detestations have a Roman holiday. You wake up feeling tetchy in the morning. You see your clerical collar hanging on a hook. 'How the hell did I get into this?' you ask. 'How the hell can I get out?' If you lose your job, you lose your house, you lose your reputation: you may even lose your wife. Have you the right to sacrifice your family to your conscience? If conscience it is, and not the devil in disguise. Plenty are waiting to convince you it is in fact the devil. Perhaps you should be patient, show humility, wait for guidance; perhaps you need a holiday. Perhaps you should see a psychiatrist. Anyway, do nothing rash: you may square the circle yet. It may seem impossible: but with God nothing is impossible. Or is it? Can God give a man the strength to be a liar?'

The Clerical Collar

20

'There goes a man who thinks it wrong to be immoral. Being immoral means having an orgasm with anybody that you are not married to. Or even wanting it, though wanting it is not so bad as getting it.

The people you could be married to are limited. You cannot be married to your father or your mother, to your brother or your sister, to your daughter or your son. After that, it becomes a bit more complicated. Look it up in the Book of Common Prayer.

You cannot be married to a person of your own sex or yourself. Homosexuality is out, therefore; and so is masturbation. If, by some kink of your personality, you get an orgasm by riding on a swing, you must keep away from swings. But if you find yourself on a swing against your will and the orgasm comes, you must fight against it. If it comes in spite of that it's just bad luck, like being raped.

There goes a man who believes that Jesus Christ was perfect. He was not immoral. He did not marry anybody, either; Jesus, therefore, never had an orgasm—unless it was against his will. But Jesus had a mighty will, so this is pretty well unthinkable. If he could turn the water into wine and control the winds and waves, then surely he could control his physical desires?

Well, not all of them. For example, he ate and drank and slept. But you have to, or you die: sex is different. You don't have to give in to go on living. You can control yourself. If a yogi can control his physical reactions to the extent of lying on a bed of nails, can we doubt that Jesus could withstand the temptations of the flesh?

That man could not doubt it, anyway; or he would not wear that kind of collar round his neck'.

21

I sat down this morning in a bath that was too hot. The sudden, scalding shock of it took me back to early childhood: to that first experience of agony and terror which lies at the root of so much of our religion. This is the taste of hell. Would any betrayal be too shameful, any surrender too abject, if it could redeem us from this awful possibility?

Hell, in a sense, is here already: you do not have to wait till you are dead. Being boiled or buried alive, being locked up in a cupboard or a coffin, having half your face blown off by a plastic bomb–these things actually happen. We are living in that sort of universe, and the revelation is a shock.

Yes, say the priests, it is that kind of universe. God made it; and, unless you do what you are told by God you will be boiled, burnt, plasticated, suffocated for ever and for ever. Their authority for saying this may seem questionable to the mind of an adult; but to a child the mere possibility is bad enough. Better take no chances: better do what this bogey man called God has said. Be good, i.e. be obedient. Do not lie, do not look at dirty pictures; go to church.

if you do that you will go.

The First Revelation

22

The first revelation is the world you live in. The world, to begin with, is your mother and yourself; and, to begin with, you cannot tell the two apart. You become aware (before you are born perhaps) that there are nice and nasty things about the world. The nice things seem to love you and you love them back. The nasty seem to hate you, and you hate them back. You trust the nice, but you do not trust the nasty. You trust your mother; for she is the chief and safest source of what is nice.

But what if she should let you down: change from being nice to nasty? What if the source of food, security and all delight should deny you food and safety: hurt, instead of giving pleasure?

Then you cannot trust her; you cannot trust the world: you cannot trust anything. All you are left with is your needs and your desires, stretching out towards a void. You stand on a precipice: the world is an empty gulf, threatening to pull you down. A mouth of horror, that will eat you up alive. There is nothing left to trust.

Can it happen? It does. It may not be your mother's fault. It may happen before the moment of your birth. You may be orphaned, metaphorically, in the womb. Or it may come later. Unless something comes to catch and mother you, you will fall into the mouth of what is nasty. You will die.

Something may come to mother you in time to keep you living, physically. But, emotionally, you may keep on falling. You grow up giddily: you cannot trust your footing any more. Your sense of balance, your security, will remain precarious. Even physically, it may be, you will feel horrified by any parable of what you dread: a precipice, for example. You may be afraid of heights. Or you may be afraid of love. You may be physically impotent, or frigid. You may be autistic.

Distrusting all otherness, you may turn in on yourself: seeking within you, that mothering, that reassurance which you fear no otherness can ever give.

Can you be cured? Can your shattered confidence in otherness be mended? Can you be taught to love and trust in other people: to defy your vertigo and make the necessary leap? Probably; but it will not be easy. I say 'probably' because the healing forces in any organism are immense. Because there is beauty, kindness and good fellowship in the world of otherness to rally the inner hope, the inner need to be made whole.

Yet the cure may never be complete. Under the loving, confident or capable exterior there may be an ever-present danger of relapse.

Who am I describing? Everybody, more or less. There are degrees of danger ranging from 0.001 per cent (or less, if you are lucky) to 9.99 per cent. Some collapse; most survive. To survive efficiently is to achieve what we call 'normality'.

Survival will depend on what kind of pressures we may be subjected to, on what lucky re-inforcements we may get, from within or from without, just in the nick of time. What I call 'luck' some may call the grace of God. Whatever name you call it by, it is unpredictable.

> *When past bearing is our grief,*
> *God the Lord will send relief.*

So sing the children in 'Hansel and Gretel'. I would like to believe it; but in terms of the individual life, it seems to me, the relief may come too late.

People do go mad; sanity, confidence, morale do crack. That may not be the end of the story; indeed, I must believe that it is not, or my own trust in the goodness and mercy of reality (or 'God', if you like) would crack as well. 'My God, why have you forsaken me?' would be the final epitaph.

For the individual life, it may sometimes seem to be; yet I believe that the individual life, extinguished on a cross or in a padded cell or in the gas filled room of the suicide, is not the totality of what is going on in each of us. I believe it is the mask, lucky or unlucky, or a larger life; which in the end, will restore, redeem and rehabilitate all that is mangled and demoralised.

Why do I believe it? Not because of what the Gospels say (though I do find these a great encouragement) but because, in my bones, I feel it would be unjust if it were otherwise.

Why should I expect justice of reality, of 'God'? Because I am made like that. This also is a revelation: that I am made like that. I cannot get behind it: it is part of that first revelation which I call 'the world itself'.

Time

Joel
2.25

23

Time is real, yes. But we have a haunting sense that time is not real in the way it seems to be, that we are under some kind of delusion, that all that has ever been is somewhere still, if only we could find it—and, perhaps all that ever will be. That by our free choice we travel one of an infinite number of possibilities; that all these others are 'there' too, waiting to be discovered somehow. Though the mind boggles at the implications of this, an intuition (or maybe just a wish, or fear) tells us that something like this must be happening. There is a pattern which we cannot see; but if we could (we feel) all our problems about free will and predestination would be cleared up. Meanwhile we proceed by faith or instinct: we act as if we were free agents, even though deterministic logic seems to leave no room for liberty at all. Unless it is the liberty of the creator of the universe, who set all things into motion. Unless he (or she, or it) is living in each of us, here and now, then we have none. But if that creator is, then not only are we free, but the creation is still going on: we participate in it, we are creators also, to the extent that we are free.

He shall restore to thee the years which the locust has eaten

BEYOND

the parable of

PERSONALITY

or   The Christ
of music

24

Music is my best friend. People alter and don't want you any more but music never lets you down.
a schoolgirl, on Television.

Whatever comes to you with the power of a personality, of a more than human personality, and says to you 'your sins are forgiven' is a kind of Jesus.

How can there be a more than human personality? Well, there is music for a start. A song can soothe, enlighten, reconcile: it can affect you like the love between two persons or the love between a group of persons. Yet a song is not a person.

What is a person, anyway? A person is a living mask by which we can see what is invisible: a body, by which we touch the intangible. A person is a kind of sacrament: something made of molecules by which we become aware of something else which is not made of molecules. Living flesh and blood are like the holy bread and wine which, according to the Catholics, are truly bread and wine, yet something more than bread and wine. They become a bridge between us and that life beyond all life which a Christian would identify with Christ, or God. With that life, by means of these simple elements, we can communicate.

Just as the consecrated bread and wine, for those who can believe in it, enable us to feed on what is neither bread nor wine; so notes of music, which are purely physical vibrations beating on the ear drum, may carry a burden which is not physical at all, though we may only find it through the physical.

Neither bread nor wine nor notes of music constitute a human personality: yet they are like one, in a way. It would be possible to reverse the metaphor: to say that what moves us, in a human personality, is really a kind of music. That a human personality is really a kind of parable in which we meet what is more than personal: the life beyond the life, or the song beyond the song.

We meet it through a multitude of parables: yet first and foremost through the parable of human beings and the relationships which are possible between them. Child and mother are the first and basic parable: a parable so powerful that we can never quite forget it. Our understanding of all later parables, our ability to receive or to reject them, will be coloured by the way we meet this early parable. The Catholic Church, with a sure instinct, has given the image of the child and mother a central place among the ikons which are used to enable us to grasp reality. Protestants lean more towards that other image; the crucifixion of the child. Both are true. They seem to contradict each other. How to reconcile them is the problem for all of us. To believe that they can be reconciled is to believe, in effect, in some kind of resurrection and ascension: not so much of the body of Jesus Christ or the believer, as of that early hope and trust which has been crucified.

To be able to believe in this, even though you call yourself an atheist, is to share the Christian hope and faith. Christians and atheists alike might be shocked at such a statement. Christians are conditioned to believe that such faith is ineffective and impossible unless you can do it through the Christian mythology which is guaranteed (they claim) by certain historical events. Atheists are counter-conditioned to believe that Christians, because they believe in what the atheist would call a lie, cannot really understand the basic nature of reality.

Both are blinded by their attachment to particular symbols. They fail to see how truth can come through any channels but the ones by which it comes to them.

In practice, though, if not in theory, they may travel the same road together. They may be united by devotion to new symbols which express the same reality for both.

God is not nice
God is not an uncle
God is an earthquake
– Hassidic saying

Psalm

25

I have been reading the Old Testament. I like it.

The picture it gives of you, O Lord, is not flattering: but it rings true.

It says that you are terrifying: there can be no doubt of that.

It says that you are jealous, and take revenge. Genocide means nothing to you. Wipe out all the Amalakites, man, woman and child: that is what you told King Saul to do. According to the Book of Kings.

I cannot admire this, as a Christian pacifist: but it is at least honest. God, you are not mealy-mouthed: you call a spade a spade.

You are arbitrary: you do just what you like, says the Old Testament. What you do is always good, because 'Good' is nothing but a description of what you do. You are utterly free. You make up morality. In fact, you make everything.

You are a maker, first and foremost. I like that. You made man in your own image, says the Old Testament. I like that. You intend that I should be a maker, yes?

At your peril, says the Old Testament. Alright then: at my peril.

No graven image can be made of you, say the Ten Commandments. Not even by the voice. There is no way of naming you, except indirectly.

The man who thinks he has you under control is in for a big surprise. There is no way to trick, manipulate or bend you to my will.

Your will alone is what has brought me into being. If I defy it, I commit suicide.

There is no way whatever to evade you: whatever I am, wherever I go to, is part of what you are.

You are my life, and when I die the life goes back to where it came from.

No pie is promised in the sky for me. What happens after death is a mystery. But you go on. Take it, or leave it (but you have to take it, in the end). Like it, or lump it. These are your terms.

You are not a Christian, Lord, in the Old Testament. You are not like Mrs Whitehouse. You are not even like St Francis, you are much more like King David.

You forbid adultery, but do not command your worshippers to be monks. Quite the opposite, in fact.

You are generous and bad tempered (though you can 'repent' of this). You enjoy yourself, you have your favourites.

The great thing about you is that you are powerful and full of life. You do what you like. Nobody can tie you down, nobody can catch you in the net of a name or image. You are open-ended, infinite.

You are terrifying; but you are exhilarating.

teach
us
to
play

Puritans
&
Players

26

'Christianity is art', wrote William Blake. 'Christianity is art, not money'.

What is art? Art is a way of doing something: painting pictures, boxing, making chairs or healing people who are sick. Christianity, says Blake, is a way of doing something: living, thinking, seeing, acting. Few Christians would disagree.

All art is *making*. All making necessitates a kind of faith. You see what is not there, except in the mind's eye, the imagination, and work in such a way that what was invisible, intangible, inaudible is given shape in time and space. What is produced will be apparent to the senses: a painting, a poem or good health instead of sickness.

Art is not to be confused, however, with the object or effect that it produces. Art is not a painting or a piece of sculpture. What art dealers buy and sell are works of art, not art itself. Works of art are a form of property.

Just as art is not the same thing as works of art, so religion is not to be confused with the objects and effects which it produces such as Bibles, doctrines or churches. That I think is what Blake meant by saying that religion is not money.

Money is essentially an object, something which you have and hold, or think you do. Your banknotes or stocks and shares may lose their value if you are unlucky; but what you hope is that your treasure will be incorruptible.

Christianity, says Blake, is not like that. Religion is like love; you cannot buy it, sell it or keep it in a bank. You cannot possess it; you can only be possessed. You can only be in it or out of it. To get in and stay in requires the same attitude as the pursuit of art. You must work at it, and yet relax. Waiting, listening, surrendering yourself to a possibility is as much a part of art as it is of religion.

Art is essentially a giving out, and not a raking in; yet, like religion, it means accepting gratefully what is offered. But if you try to bank it, if you try to lock it up like gold ingots in Fort Knox,

you are in danger of losing it. If you feel you have the title deeds to love, salvation, forgiveness or any of the things which religion is about, you are mistaken. They are not worth the paper they are written on.

WHAT I KEPT I HAVE LOST
WHAT I GAVE THAT I HAVE

Did not David dance before
the Ark?

Truth & Play

David daunced himself alone
without either women or
musicall Instruments to
effeminate the minde
                    Phillip Stubbes
ANATOMIE OF ABUSES 1583

27

To tell the truth, said Oscar Wilde, you have to wear a mask. A puritan like Philip Stubbes would disagree. His instinctive distrust of the theatre springs from a crude, half-baked conception of the truth. He thinks that you can tell it straight. For certain purposes you can. 'The cat sat on the mat'. Either the cat did sit there, or he didn't. But there are other kinds of truth which you cannot take hold of so easily. Language is riddled with all kinds of ambiguity. If anyone says 'God' or 'Folk' or 'moral', you need to know exactly what he means when he is saying it. He could mean a hundred things. And the higher up you go, the thicker grows the mystery. We must learn to live with this.

Music is one way of doing it. Music has no words, so it can tell no truth or lies. Music can bear witness to the mystery and that is all. Music, in a sense, is absolutely silent. From this point of view, Quakers are the most musical of all the sects.

Song is not pure music. Song has words. Song is none the worse for that, but it raises special problems. I shall leave them for the moment.

Drama is another way of doing it. In a drama, all characters should be regarded as fictitious. Few people are capable of doing this. If historical characters are introduced–Jesus Christ, or Winston Churchill–you are immediately in trouble. You are handling two kinds of truth at once: the truth of art, and the truth of history. (I don't say you should not do it; only that you are in trouble.)

Drama has something of the character of music. It plays with archetypal realities: with super-reality, rather than the reality of daily life. Here it is the super-real which must wear a mask: the mask of everyday realities. The characters must talk and act sufficiently like human beings for the thing to grip: even if (as in Greek and Christian drama) the characters are gods, or goddesses.

Both music and drama have another thing in common: those who present them are described as 'players'. There is a certain type of mind to which all forms of play are suspect. It can only approve of games as a form of exercise or as training in the skills required for 'real life'. Any other kind of play (and this includes most art) is thought of as idle, frivolous or insincere.

At the other extreme you have the Hindu point of view which sees the whole creation as a form of play. Why else should 'God' want to make it, anyway? Things are 'useful' in relation to something else: but finally there has to be something which is an end in itself. The aim of man's existence, according to the catechism, is to 'praise God and enjoy Him for ever'. Is that not a kind of play?

I see all human play as a foreshadowing of this. As a foretaste, here and now, is what a Christian may expect. Furthermore, I see all play *as a way of finding out the truth.* This is true of art; it is true of mechanical invention and of mathematics too. You push it this way and you push it that, for no reason you can see: for the pure heaven or the hell of it. Suddenly, by doing this, you see a new relationship, a hidden possibility. You make a poem, or a spinning jenny, or Einstein's theory of relativity.

And all this goes for sex as well. Procreation may or may not be the prime end of sexual activity. But, even if it were, it would be a coldblooded procreator who could get no fun or joy from what he did. Even the churches are now beginning to acknowledge this. To celebrate the fact, and not deplore it. Let nobody tell me that *they always did.* They might have, in theory. In practice, they were scared to death of sex; and most of them still are.

So (to return to song) I take my stand on the side of the players against Puritans like Philip Stubbes (whether Protestant, Catholic, Marxist or Capitalist) who would permit no celebration but the singing of a psalm, taken from the text of whatever Bible they permit. Such people will permit no playing with the truth. The truth has been infallibly stated. Further experiment can only lead to heresy. This doctrine I regard as diabolical, and the god it serves as a devil in disguise, whatever name they call him by: Jehovah, The Church, the Party, History or even Jesus.

Otherness

28

Born with a body, you are not complete. From the otherness around you, food must first be taken in. You will die without it. You need shelter, warmth and friendly contact. You need love, for want of a better word. The first way you get love is by getting nourishment, by being played with and protected. The otherness, on which you must depend for this, is part of what you are: quite literally so, to start with. Your mother's body is your own; her blood-stream and your own are one.

Even when your bodies have been separated, you are still bound by your necessity: if not to your mother (for she may have died) then someone else. Whatever feeds, plays with and protects you is your mother from now on: whether a she-wolf, as in the case of Romulus and Remus, or Dr Lorenz, as in the case of the goslings which he writes about. This large, whiskered, protective moving object was for them that friendly shape of otherness which, to most of us, is designated by the name of mother.

The Madonna and the Child are a symbol for all of us. We come out of otherness, and we must be carried by it: if we cannot we shall die. This is physically true: it is emotionally true, as well. If we are nourished physically but cannot, for one reason or another, learn to trust that otherness, we are nipped in the bud. We are emotionally dead, or not yet born; we may end on the gallows, or in a lunatic asylum. Or we may become a head of state, and massacre a million people. But we shall be stunted still; we shall not have learned to live with otherness.

We cannot stay forever in the arms of the Madonna, or Dr Lorenz. Physically, we must travel on; but there is a sense in which we must, emotionally, love and trust that otherness as we did at the beginning. If we cannot, we are lost. The image may change from the Madonna to a Father God, or no God: that does not matter. What matters is our attitude. If we cannot love and lean on otherness, we are cut adrift. We are like that convict in *Les Misérables*, sinking lonely in the sea, with the warmth and safety that we long for mocking us, and sailing cruelly away.

But physically, we must get out of our mother's arms and learn to love our otherness in more sophisticated ways. We must learn to fight with our environment: perhaps to kill and eat it. Or be killed and eaten. That has been the fate of millions of sheep and cattle, and now and then a missionary. How can we love this otherness, which may even crucify us?

Yet that is what we have to do: hang on the cross, in one way or another, and, at the same time, keep on rocking in the cradle. Is this impossible? It may be so: but if it is, I see no hope for any of us. We are mocked by our own reality: our creation is diabolical. Is this possible? It may be; and at moments that is how it looks.

Yet in love (and not love only, but the joy of conflict too) the hope of an atonement, an at-one-ment, between the cradle and the cross, seems to be foreshadowed. In love, in conflict, in creation, we are turning inside out. The crucifixion of the self, of that identity which is bounded by the body, becomes the cradle of another kind of self. We are not the child alone: we are the madonna too. We cradle our otherness: the thing we dread has become the thing we love. We die, for otherness: by doing so; we save the self. We lose one life, to keep another. By the passion of creation, love or fighting we can make a leap into that larger environment of which our doomed and blinkered private life is just a part.

Why does this have to be? What is the object of the exercise? Why put us into private bodies (assuming that there is a putter) in the first place? This is the kind of question which Buddha called 'unprofitable'. You are in a burning house, he says. The only important question is: how do I get out of it? Or, in Christian and Hebraic phraseology 'What must I do to be saved?'

This was the question which the young man put to Jesus: and he already had the answer, in theory at any rate: 'Thou shalt love the Lord thy God with all thy heart, and all thy strength, and all thy mind: and thy neighbour as thyself'. You could rephrase that as follows: You must love the source of your own self (whether you picture it as a Father, a Mother, Dr Lorenz or Ultimate Reality) and love it where you meet it: in your self, or other creatures, for it is the same in both.

To say it is easy: to do it is another. What Jesus added to what the young man knew already, was a practical suggestion. 'Sell all you have and give it to the poor, and follow me'. For the young man, that could have been the right suggestion; but Jesus varied his suggestion with the case. To the woman taken in adultery, he suggested something else.

Whether they followed his suggestions or not (and the young man apparently did not), there would have been no point in making them but for one fact: they fitted in with what his listeners knew or suspected already (however dimly or unconsciously)—namely, that the other (even as enemy) is part of the self: that you can only save your life by losing it. This knowledge, hope or suspicion is in the very bones of all creation: not only in men but in lions and tigers too, even the invertebrates. They fight and kill; but they also reproduce and die for their own progeny, or for the herd, the gang or species. The ability to respond to this suggestion is, I think, what Jesus meant by 'faith'. Some may have more of it than others: but without it, nothing Jesus ever said or did could have meant anything to anybody.

What Jesus gave us, by his life and death, was a working Image of the way things really are. Whether we can trust the Gospels as true history or not, this Image has a healing power. Like a certain kind of dream, it confronts us with the truth of our own situation, which is this: that cradled by otherness; we are also crucified by otherness. What are we to do about it? Cut our throats, and wish that it had never happened? Or listen to the faith in us, and do what seems impossible: turn the cross we carry inside out, be born into and cradled by that otherness of which we are a part? (Or of which, by loving and by being loved, we can feel, as well as know, we are a part?) Is this really possible? We hope it is. The banner of our hope, this is what the gospel carries: only faith can follow it. There is no proof in documents, in big black Bibles. All they do is to unfold the flag.

Matthew, Mark, Luke and John could all be liars: the flag flies, in spite of that. How did it ever get here? Never mind. 'Belief', in one sense, is immaterial. For as Jesus said (or is said to have said) 'The devils also believe, and tremble'. Faith is what you have to have. If you can have faith without belief, good luck to you. By faith you embrace the otherness: carried by and carrying creation, you create.

One is one
and all alone
and evermore
shall be so !

alone ?

In that one
there is Another
In that I
there is a you.
Holy is the
one for ever
Holy is the
other too.

A Sporting God

The Demon Bowler at
The Christian Wicket

GOD'S LOYAL
OPPOSITION

For when the One Great Scorer comes to write against your name
He marks — not that you won or lost But how you played the game.
Grantland Rice
1880 — 1954

Is creation a disaster?

Would it be better for all concerned if it had never happened? After pain, oblivion is such a blessing that it seems a pity ever to have broken it.

Who broke it? Who created? Who is responsible?

No one, says the atheist. Things just are. But why? He doesn't know.

God created it, the Christians say (and the Moslem, and the Jew). God is good: so the creation is a good idea. What we are living in, the fact that we can live at all, is no disaster.

The atheist need not agree. Not believing in a god, let alone a good one, he is not obliged to be an optimist. He may be an optimist, but he does not have to justify the fact. The atheist has no theology.

The Christian has, and the toughest problem of theology is this; if God is good, wise, and almighty, why has he created pain?

No one can answer it. Some Christians try, but their attempts are not impressive. For example: 'there would be no pleasure if there, were no pain'. That may be the case, in the universe we know. Was it beyond the will of God to create a universe where crucifixion was unnecessary? If so, why didn't he?

Why did he have to create anything?

Two answers seem possible:
1. That he couldn't help it.
2. That he did it for fun.

If 1. is true, God is subject to necessity. Who makes necessity, if not God? So 1. is a non-starter. That leaves 2.

If God made the world for fun (a non-Christian might reply) he may be mighty, but he is not good. He is a monster.

If God is a monster, then we have another problem: why has he created Goodness? The non-Christian might reply (turning the Christian answer upside down) that there can be no evil without good. You must have pleasure, joy and hope to dangle in front of man: otherwise he cannot be frustrated.

The idea of a bad god offers as many problems as the idea of a good god. So what about a god who is neither bad nor good? A god who scatters pain and pleasure to keep creation on its toes, running from the stick and to the carrot?

Such a god is thinkable: or, at least as far as any God (or absence of God) is thinkable. But what could his motive be?

To amuse himself? One might live in terror of a god like this, but I see no reason for loving him.

But, if this God is not just watching, but playing in the game himself—living in all creatures (but self handicapped, so that not a single creature realises that he, she or it is really God)—then the proposition is more interesting. Such a god might be considered whimsical, but not cold blooded. He can take the knocks that he is giving: he displays a sporting spirit.

No Moslem or Jew would accept a God like that: his utter otherness is an article of faith. No Christian would accept it either—excepting in the case of Jesus. Here, God suffers in the person of a creature. He is crucified.

When Christians claim that he rose from the dead and ascended into heaven, they attribute to this human a privilege not accorded to the others: especially if they insist that he knew that this would happen. Millions have hung on crosses without his happy ending to look forward to. Only if God in Jesus did not know for sure that he was God, did not know that he would rise again, was he really playing fair.

If that is what he did, however, then he was behaving as Alan Watts would claim is the way he is behaving all the time, in every creature that he has created, right down to an earthworm or an atom.

If God is present in all creatures, Jesus is no longer unique, but typical: not only of mankind, but creation as a whole. The atonement between God and man is not achieved by Jesus, but revealed. He shows us, by the image of his words and acts, the way things really are.

To return to the first question: is creation a disaster? If it is, then we are not the only ones in trouble. God is suffering as well, for we are nothing but the blinkered, hoodwinked, fragments of that God ourselves. God, presumably, knows what he is doing in this game of God, where we are players on the field. Dare one imagine another fragmentation of the unity of God sitting, unblinkered, in the Pavilion: and shall we, when this fascinating but often horrifying game is over, join him there at last and be allowed to see what creation is about?

This idea of creation as a game or drama, with God acting all the parts owes more to Hinduism than to Christianity. Yet it has a curiously British flavour. One thinks not only of the cricket field, but of Shakespeare: 'All the world's a stage, and all the men and women are the players'. The Victorians (orthodox in this at least) tended to see God in the Umpire or the Scorer, rather than the players on the field. Shakespeare came much closer to the Hindu point of view. As a dramatist, he too was a creator of a kind, living a fragmented life in all the characters which he created: Shakespeare is behaving like the God of the Hindus.

The image of a sporting and dramatic God may offend those brought up in the Biblical tradition. To those who have rejected that tradition, it may be more acceptable than the Garden of Eden and that fatal apple. The headmaster-like God of the Old Testament is out of favour. The playful god of India, masking from himself his own identity, seems a more complex and more modern character.

Jesus still hangs there, like a question mark. To call him the Lamb of God, who takes away the sins of the world, is to speak a language few can understand today. We may get more help from the Veda than from the Old Testament or the Apostle's Creed in giving our own contemporary answer to that question mark.

I know I hung
for nine nights on a tree
blown by the wind and
wounded with a spear
a sacrifice to Odin.
I myself
was offered to myself
upon that tree
the roots of which
no man can ever tell
none gave me food or drink
As I looked down
I saw the runes and
shrieking took them up
And then fell back again.

The Poetic Eddas

From the tail end

30

I take my text from Brian Silcock, writing about the flat-worm in *The Sunday Times*:

' ... the flat-worm in question reproduces itself by dividing into two, the front and back halves both eventually becoming complete worms. In the United States Tom Sonneborn kept the lines derived from front and rear halves separate, and he found that the former died out eventually, while the latter survived indefinitely. It is the head end which contains the worm's brain, and in this line the non-multiplying brain cells would not get replaced. Worms derived from the tail ends, on the other hand, have to grow new brains. J. B. S. Haldane once drily remarked that this demonstrated the mortality of the soul and the immortality of the body'.

Faith, hope and charity are like three organs of a single virtue. Though one of them may cease to function, the organism may survive by virtue of the other two—for a while, at any rate. When faith is gone, we may still get by on hope and charity.

Faith, which we in the west have tended to equate with mere belief, is in poor shape at the moment. But if hope and love survive something like a faith will still be operating, though we may not call it that. The divided flat-worm will still reproduce itself, from one end or from the other.

But one end is more basic than the other. The tail end is the equivalent of love, perhaps, which can reproduce *ad infinitum*. Faith and hope are not so hardy. Credal statements come, not from the tail, but from the head.

2001
A.D.

film directed by kubrick
from the book by A. C. Clarke

31

You need to go to this film twice. The first time you are looking for the usual landmarks which will tell you where you are, what to expect. That tall, black, oblong monolith, for example, which is so puzzling to the prehistoric apes. (And for the viewer.) Only man, surely, could shape something so rectangular? Could it be that we are *not* in prehistoric times, as we imagined? Never mind, you think: we shall be told. But we are not. Later, the monolith is discovered on the moon. How did it get there? Your guess is as good as mine. Later, it appears to be floating in deep space; by this time, you have given up expecting anything to be explained. Good: you are learning. Far more distressing is what happens to the astronauts, locked out of their space-craft by a computer with a one-track mind. Things look bad; but surely there will be a happy ending? At first it looks as though there will. Taking off in a globular module from the mother ship, an astronaut pursues and grabs his locked-out companion as he goes whirling off into infinity. But how can they get back into the mother ship? The computer will not let them in. Then, breaking all the rules of film heroics, the one surviving astronaut abandons his companion. (Why, is he dead? If so, it's all right: but you want to know.) Alone, he drives on in his module; but with what in view? To Saturn? Is that where all these terrifying, beautiful, psychedelically coloured landscapes are? Or has he blown his mind? Finally, amazingly, we see him walking in his space-suit, through an elegantly furnished, greenish apartment, with eighteenth century engravings on the walls. He looks into a mirror, sees that he is wrinkled. Later, we see him in a dressing gown, eating the sort of meal you get upon a Jumbo Jet. Still later, even older, completely bald by now, he is lying on a bed. Dying? And then, out of a final whirl, the figure of a human foetus, visibly living, waiting to be born.

The audience files out, in silence. Well, what could you say? This, to put it mildly, is not what anybody could expect. It was beautiful to look at, but shatteringly unconsoling. Worst of all, it left you with a chilly feeling that it could be true: that no cosy happy ending was to be expected, that man might in fact be on his own in empty space, with nobody to give an answer. That this was the crucifixion we were born for.

Put like that, it sounds entirely negative; yet it was not. For one thing the sheer power and majesty of the panoramic views seemed to dwarf all human expectations. There was a kind of holiness about the horror (about *all* horror, perhaps, when you come to think of it). Man was reduced to nothing: yet the might and splendour, which seemed so careless of his happiness, went on. Maybe Moses felt that way about Jehovah. You could expect nothing from him in the way, for example, of an after life. All that you could do was fear and worship. Here, perhaps, was the old, original, religous shiver. If there was anything to be hoped for—not expected—for the individual worshipper, any sort of resurrection, it could only come from the complete destruction of what he was already. All his categories of awareness had to be completely shattered first. As a butterfly, the caterpillar might survive: but would he remember what he was before? God knows. With or without a resurrection, he must go down first into the dark. Praising or protesting, he must die.

Death, loneliness, annihilation: that is what this film is really about. What we are most afraid to think of, this film faces with a stoical steadiness: almost a nobility. It is as religious, as pre-Christian, as the Iliad. It sees the beauty, the splendour, the longing which we know, which are undoubtably there, against the background of the dark.

Pre-Christian, yes: but can we ever be Christian unless we have been pre-Christian first? Can we ever see what the Christian answer is about, unless we have learned to ask the pagan question? Unless we have faced the possibility that this life may be all there ever is and that we shall have to leave it—perhaps in anxiety, disgrace or terror? Or in physical agony, as Jesus did? Perhaps the shallowness of much Christianity arises from the fact that we have stifled our anxiety, never really learned to face it. We sing ourselves a lullaby we never quite believe in: we distract ourselves by looking at a pretty picture. We use our Christianity as dope; we never really face the possibility that it could be something else. Not a way of evading horror, but of facing and transmuting horror: of finding our saving truth in the very heart of what we dread the most. That, surely, is what the Cross is all about. We do not like to think of Jesus on the cross: the Jesus who cried 'My God, why hast thou forsaken me?' The Jesus who, however much he may have trusted God, could not know exactly what would happen next: only that he must go down, alone; as all men do. Or do we imagine a Jesus who was absolutely sure that everything would be alright; as soon as this unpleasant business of the crucifixion had been finished? That, I think, is what many Christians do imagine. If they are right, it puts Jesus in a very privileged position, compared to any other human being who has ever lived. It makes him more a god, but less a man: for he did not really suffer as a man must suffer.

He was like a rich man's son working his way through college or sleeping on a park bench, safe in the knowledge that his father was a millionaire and that he'd soon be back in the Rolls Royce again, with commissionaires opening the door for him. The only Jesus who is any good to us is a Jesus who could really taste our doubt and terror, who could really feel the horror and abandonment of being cut loose, like that astronaut, in outer space. If he could face all that and come up with an answer, then it might apply to us.

The trouble with the Jesus story is that we *know* it had a happy ending: that is what the Gospels say, at any rate. Can you ever really share the agony of a man who is hanging on a cliff if you *know* (because you've seen this film before) that the Coast Guards are on the way? If you are used to seeing that kind of film, you come to almost any film with a false optimism. Well, A.D. 2001 lets you down badly; but, because of this false optimism, you are shielded from the horror till the end. You never really share the desperation of the astronauts until long after they have begun to feel it. You are cheered up by false signposts. That is why you should see it a second time and get the full force of its uncomfortable message. And perhaps it might help us to participate more fully in the feeling of Jesus and his followers if somebody could make a film called, say A.D. 33 in which things do not turn out happily at all. No resurrection, no ascension: only the body in the tomb, exactly as expected. The disciples all go back to their old jobs: Peter fishing, Matthew collecting taxes. Saul, the Pharisee, will never change his name to Paul. The New Testament will not be written.

Who would bother to make such a film, however? Not the Christians; they are committed to the Resurrection. As for the non-Christians, why should they bother? Not even the Russian Communists, at the height of their anti-God campaign, felt that it was worth the trouble.

Yet, as we turn into the nineteen-seventies, the impossible occurs: Jesus is rescued by the unbelievers. Dennis Potter in *Son of Man,* Tim Rice in *Jesus Christ Superstar* crack their way into the Christian legend like a couple of grave-robbers. The story, as

they tell it ends with the Crucifixion. Freed from the gilded sepulchre to which the faithful have consigned him by their wonder, love and praise, Jesus emerges as a human being.

By killing Jesus (you might say), by denying his resurrection, they have enabled him to come alive. The Jesus who walked on water and rose up from the dead (even if he *did* rise from the dead, which none can prove or disprove now)—is, for this generation almost impossible to believe in literally. Yet this is the Jesus which the orthodox proclaimed.

Is there no way for Jesus to speak to the condition of such as these but to shed the miracles which he did or did not do, to die like any other man or woman, *and not to rise up from the dead*? The Jesus who comes down from his home in heaven, has a bad time on earth but then goes safely back to heaven, does not mean a thing to them. They just don't believe he did it. Perhaps only the Jesus who is still in trouble, who hangs like an unanswered question on the cross, speaks to them in a language which they understand. The most moving, the most truly contemporary song in *Jesus Christ Superstar* is the one in which Mary Magdalene tells the second person of the Trinity not to worry *(Everything's Alright)*. Contemporary? Yes: but it has a mediaeval flavour, too. Think, for example, of *Adam lay y-bounden* which ends with the statement that it is a lucky thing that Adam *did* take the apple or we should not have had the Virgin Mary.

Not the Christ who has risen, but the Christ who has not risen yet, who may never rise unless we help him: the forsaken Christ whom Mother Teresa meets in the outcasts of Calcutta—this is the Christ who still has power to attract. You do not have to be Christian to be attracted.

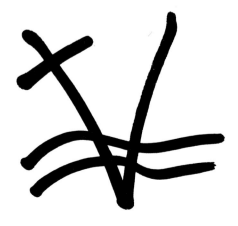

When at any time my condition was veiled, my secret belief was stayed firm, and hope underneath held me as an anchor in the bottom of the sea, anchoring my immortal soul to its Bishop, causing it to swim above the sea, the world where all raging waves, foul weather, tempests and temptations are. I saw also that there was an ocean of darkness and death, but an infinite ocean of light and love, which flowed over the ocean of darkness.   GEORGE FOX.

playing back the resurrection

32

Through the window of a dream you look into another world where things are not articulated in the way that we are used to. Present, past and future leapfrog over one another. Near and far cannot be relied upon to keep their proper distance, as they do in waking life. You can be in two places at once. Relationships are seen and developments occur, but not according to the rules of time and place.

Waking you may remember, vividly or dimly, that something important has been happening. To describe it to yourself or to another you are driven to construct a kind of story. You must re-articulate your non-temporal, non-spatial experience in terms of tenses: you must separate what is here from what is there.

Not only in sleep, but sometimes when you are awake, you are caught up in an experience which has the qualities of dreamtime, in that it makes nonsense of our daylight categories. You do not doubt the reality of what has happened; but how to express it, excepting by a parable; you cannot see. What you write down, or recount, is more of an *aide mémoire* than a representation of what has happened: a kind of musical notation which only you can play back properly.

Reading the gospel accounts of the Resurrection, I get the feeling that something like this happened to the Apostles. We are left with the musical notation, but we don't know how to play it.

For a fresh way of looking at the Resurrection, see Stephen Verney's INTO THE NEW AGE, a Fontana paperback.

Cowper is mad
and
Abelard

ABAILARDUS
AMAT
HELOISAM

33

Hymnwriters are like clowns in one respect: they help others when they cannot help themselves. Grimaldi, depressed, went to see a doctor without saying who he was. He was advised to go and see the clown Grimaldi. Cowper, in a lunatic asylum, needed to be assured of what he had himself written just a year before:

> God moves in a mysterious way
> His wonders to perform.

Cowper's lapse from sanity in no way invalidates the truth of what he wrote before, any more than Van Gogh's madness destroys the value of the pictures which he painted both before and after. It would be comforting to be able to believe that clowns, hymnwriters and painters always passed from darkness into light: that the graph of their moral, spiritual and mental health went ever upwards, as seems to have been the case with St Paul and St Augustine. But this was not the case with William Cowper; morally he may have soared, but mentally he kept on dipping.

With other hymnwriters the case was rather different. Did Peter Abelard write *0 quanta qualia*—so haunting in the latin, so tamely translated in the English Hymnal—before, during, or after his disastrous love affair with Héloise? And if any of the Psalms of David *are* in fact by David, what about that appalling moral lapse with regard to Bathsheba, whose husband he put in the first line of battle in order that he should be killed? Was that before or after he had written all those words we sing on Sunday?

The character of a Pot Poet
John Earle, Microcosmographie
1628

sitting in a bawdy house he writes GOD'S JUDGE-MENTS

THE ARISTOS

One morning as I was sitting by the fire, a great cloud came over me, and a temptation beset me; but I sate still. And it was said, "All things come by nature"; and the elements and stars came over me, so that in a manner I was quite clouded with it. GEORGE FOX

34

The *Aristos* by John Fowles. His disbelief in a God who could intervene or be amenable to any kind of prayer swings me into a depression. Not by the force of reason (he brings no new arguments) but by the force of a personality to which I feel akin. I am pulled by a sort of gravity, as the tides are by the moon.

This exposes the peculiar nature of that thing we call a choice: which John Fowles, as an existentialist, is much concerned with. For although each of us is separate, and forced to choose, it is a quality of each of us to be gregarious as well: to need the support, approval, company of others. Rooted in and nourished by otherness, we wilt if we are isolated.

'No man is an island'. That is a truth which seems to cross the truth of individuality. Cut off from the continent of which I am a part, my individuality becomes a horror.

Existentialism, by affirming the individual to the limit, leads to despair: for it exposes the falsity, the absurdity, the appalling paradox of his position. From this despair he is forced to make a leap of faith, or perish: whether to communism, Christianity or an instinctive kind of optimism: for (mercifully) 'cheerfulness keeps breaking through'. Or the body can come to the rescue: for the body is a blind believer, untroubled by any philosophic doubt. The counsel of the body is 'embrace some friendly form of otherness: whether in the form of food or drink or the body of a human being'.

Without faith (or the body's humble, folk equivalent) I am appalled by that ocean of otherness which I cannot control. I cannot beat it, I must join it, or I die. To be excommunicated by all otherness is, ultimately, to be cut off from the roots of what I am.

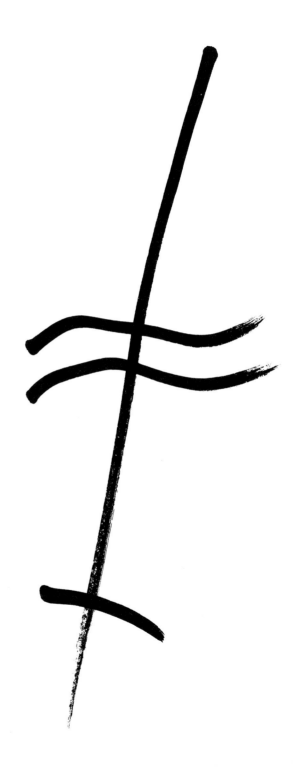

Donne
and
Herbert

John DONNE 1572-1631
George HERBERT 1593-1633

35

In a game of cards or tennis there may come a moment when you see you cannot possibly win. The same can happen with your hope of a happy marriage or a brilliant career.

Can you go on playing still, with no expectation of a win? Yes, according to the *Gita*. That is the way you should have played it from the start. Not for the victory, though you have to strive for that, but for the game itself. Playing is a form of worship.

Donne and Herbert were ambitious men. Both hoped to serve the state in some high capacity. Both were disappointed. Both became clergymen.

A cynic might conclude that they had settled for a second best. But can a second best turn out better than the first? Can defeat be met in such a way that it yields a greater prize than victory?

Most of us are destined to failure, which is a form of suffering. How to use our suffering, how to turn the lead of our defeat into the gold of something else, is the object of religious alchemy. Not the only one; but one that most of us are interested in.

late
have
I
loved
you
beauty
so
old
and
so new,
late
have
I
loved
you !

St. Augustine

patterns

Incarnation

36

Here is a chair: the incarnation of a pattern, of a possibility. It has a body made of wood. But before that wood was cut and assembled into this shape we call 'a chair', where was that possibility?

On this chair there sits the incarnation of another possibility; and this one is conscious, which the incarnation of the chair is not. Or so we assume; we may be wrong.

I am conscious, anyway, of the fact that I exist. This consciousness appears to be attached to the structure which I call 'my body'. I cannot remember any time when it was not.

From my image in a mirror or on a television screen I can see what I look like to other people, though only part of what I am is visible. My consciousness, my awareness of myself as 'I', is not visible. Yet between this consciousness and my body is a link; and when this link is severed, I am dead. The pattern I incorporated is no more: not in time and space, at any rate.

Where has it gone to, and where did it reside before I came to birth? All questions about my survival after death, or whether I have ever been alive before, are questions about the nature of a pattern. In this case, a pattern which includes the feeling that I am uniquely 'I': a feeling which all human beings seem to share. The feeling that 'I am', and that I am unique, is typical.

Though patterns may become incarnate in the four dimensions of time and space, they appear to come and go; yet even when they are not actually embodied in, say, a human being, or a table, or a chair, they must have some kind of reality. They do not exist; but they are potential, still. You might, perhaps, say that they endure or wait (you cannot say 'exist') in the dimension of potentiality.

We can apprehend a pattern that does not exist in time and place: we apprehend it, as it were, prophetically by the faculty of faith or the imagination. By labour, we give it a body in our time and space: by the construction of a chair, a table, or a song.

And so it was, and is, with Jesus: who by his life and work revealed a pattern which had been apprehended, but more dimly, by certain prophets in the past. Most clearly, perhaps, by the writers of the Book of Isaiah and the Book of Job. What Jesus revealed, embodied, communicated, was the pattern of the maker of all patterns, whom he called The Father. That is what the Christians claim, at any rate.

Jesus was crucified. What happened to the pattern then? No longer tangible and visible in time and space it hovered potentially, as it must have done from the beginning, until the time and space were right for its embodiment.

'And on the third day, He rose again, according to the Scriptures'. Most Christians have taken this to mean that the body of Jesus was reanimated and that he continued to appear to those who had known him, until He 'ascended into Heaven'.

Those who are not Christians do not feel obliged to believe all this. But even they might be willing to admit that the pattern displayed by Jesus, even in his mortal life, was not finished by the Crucifixion. Once displayed, it continued to haunt the minds and hearts of men: it has hovered over our history ever since and again become incarnate, to a greater degree or lesser, in the lives of St Paul, St Francis and innumerable men and women who were caught up, as it were, in the pattern of the dance that Jesus led them. 'Not I, but Christ is me!' said Paul.

So: Christians follow, well or ill, the dancing pattern which they find in Jesus. But is there no other way of finding it?

'Other sheep have I', said Jesus, 'which are not of this fold'. This has usually been understood to mean that the good news brought by Jesus was riot only for the sons of Abraham. Gentiles could be Christians, too.

Others might interpret it more boldly. Jesus, they might claim, meant that he would come again, in other times and places. On other stars and planets, possibly, in another shape. Not only Science Fiction writers but even theologians have welcomed such a possibility.

Some might go even further, and speculate that Jesus could have appeared again already, long before the birth of Jesus, in the form of Krishna, or the Buddha, or the White Cow Buffalo Woman of the Sioux. Such time-twisting speculations have not, so far, had the blessing of the church.

37

First, the bomb: blinding, burning, crippling the one you love. Or it could be a car crash, or the birth of a mis-shapen child.

First the shock, the unbelief; then, the agony. Then, perhaps, the fury: 'Who did this?' But there may be nobody for you to blame. God, then. But you may not believe in God.

'I wanted to meet Him face to face', said Archie Hill, 'to spit on Him, to throttle Him slowly with my own two hands. I wanted God to be real, so that I could do this to Him'. The crime of God, the God he wanted to believe in so that he could throttle Him, was a child mentally and physically handicapped.

But see what happened next: in this God-forsaken landscape, something flowered. First, the love of this boy's mother for her stricken child; next, the trust and affection of the boy himself. 'I will remember, always, the way his eyes lit up when I walked towards him'.

Archie Hill could not equate this love with 'God'—that word was still suspect. 'I put my trust in the Sacred Woman. Nature'. A surprising thing to say; but then, I remembered these words from *Piers Plowman*:

Lerne to love, quoth Kinde, and leve all other.

Kinde was not God, either; Kinde was Nature, in a sense. She stood for that natural or supernatural self-giving which is seen in the loving of a mother for her child. You could say, perhaps, that she was a face of God.

From this burning house in which, as the Buddha says, we find that we are living, we must look for an escape. Archie Hill found one way, Mary Craig another. She also had an afflicted child—two, in fact; one with Gargoylism, one a mongol. She was rescued from self-pity by the victims of a concentration camp. From them she learned how to use her suffering: it was transmuted to compassion for the suffering of others. Unlike Archie Hill, she found the image for this saving love not in Nature, but in Christ.

So, God dies; and, by dying, comes to life. The God that Archie Hill so longed to throttle was a phantom anyway: a monster created by our crooked way of looking. We forsake Him as He has forsaken us; and we are right. We have been looking with the wrong eyes, in the wrong direction. What we find instead of Him, what rescues us, we may call Love, or Christ, or Nature. We may want to call it Him or Her. Does it matter what we call it?

Perhaps it does; I am not sure. But the main thing is to find it.

Cruelty
α Lore
of God

x † x ✓   ~~you~~ I
crucify
~~me~~ you

38

'I believe in a cruel God who has made me in his image'. — . Iago, in Verdi's *Otello*.

There is cruelty, and there is love. Both, ultimately, have to be referred to God. From where could anything have come, except from God? To dwell upon the cruelty, to put our faith in it, can only lead us to despair. So we must dwell upon the love.

Epictetus puts it like this: 'Everything has two handles, one by which it may be borne, the other by which it cannot. If your brother be unjust, do not take the matter up by that handle—the handle of injustice—for that is the handle by which it cannot be taken up; but rather by the handle that he is your brother and brought up with you; and then you will be taking it up as it can be borne'.

Christ incarnates the love. Christ is the handle by which things can be taken up. And what of the cruelty? The Cross is the cruelty. The Cross is part of the creation. What its function is God only knows: but our function (say the Christians) is to take it up as Christ did. To transform it by an act of love. And that, perhaps, is what the function of the Cross is: to train us in heroic love.

This Happened

call it
nothing

39

This happened over twenty years ago.

In the Royal Hotel, Woburn Place, A. L. Lloyd was lecturing about Romanian Folk Music. Round us were showcases containing examples of embroidered shirts, and objects connected with music or agriculture. I had come alone, from Gray's Inn Road, in a state of mind that matched the weather: bleak, bone chilling. I was in trouble and could see no way out, except by a miracle. I did not believe in that kind of a miracle. I had ceased to call myself a Christian, or a pacifist. My motives for being either—or rather, of trying to be either, for I had never quite succeeded: I had lived, as it were, on the legacy of a belief which I expected shortly to inherit—my motives now seemed insufficient. I had done the wrong thing all along the line, though (it seemed to me) I could not have chosen otherwise.

A. L. Lloyd was talking about the way, in Romania, folk songs had been passed from one generation to another. A mother (did he really say this, or do I imagine it?) would teach her daughter how to sing a song, saying: 'You don't see the point or meaning of this song now, but you will need it later'. As if she were giving her a magic spell or a bottle of medicine.

Suddenly I noticed that something was happening. I no longer felt alone and clue-less; or rather, I felt that being like this did not matter for, whatever happened, I was being lifted by a kind of tide or ocean: and not only I, but all the men and women and children, probably the dogs and cats and leaves as well if they had ever thought about it. Even if we were alone, we were all alone together. This offered a kind of courage: not hope, perhaps, but comradeship. And though my personal future still seemed like a dark and narrow tunnel which I must travel into without any promise of daylight at the other end, this prospect began to feel less like a death sentence from a doctor or a judge and more like a song.

Song, I saw, was the key; and folk song in particular. Here, for me at any rate, was the spell, the medicine, which I could not understand yet which could hcal me all the same. It demanded no impossible belief in God or Jesus or the Virgin Birth; it demanded no political allegiance; it did not seem to care if you were a monk or married, a commando or a pacifist.

Still listening to A. L. Lloyd and looking at the corn-dollies I was trying to sort out this experience which I was having. I wasn't even sure, in a way that I was having it. It was like a possibility I had caught sight of, out of the corner of my eye: which might come closer, if I didn't frighten it, and declare itself to me. Even eat out of my hand (or feed me out of its hand: for it seemed a two way process).

Could this be God, creeping up on me after I had said goodbye: after I had given up banging on his Christian gateway? If so, the less I said about it the better, for the moment anyway. The important thing was not to overstate or understate: not to try to fit it into any sort of category. Above all, not to try to equate it with God, still less with the name of Jesus. If I did (I knew) a kind of blight of insincerity, of fear, of sentimentality, would spoil it all. So, call it nothing: watch it, from the corner of an eye.

anonymous